A Meditation Guide For Kids

Written by:
Taylor Harper

Illustrated by:
Frances Rose Espanol

ISBN:

978-0-578-32199-8 (sc)

Illustrations by Frances Rose Español

Layout and Design by Louie Romares

This book is dedicated to:

My son Ezra and his side kicks - you are mommy's little monsters.

Ezra (11 months), Blaze (12), and Benji (4)

If you are interested in stories with a happy ending,
this one's for you parents,
because your children will go to bed in the end.

Mantra Monster

A Meditation Guide for Kids

Hi,
I'm Mantra!

Come play with me, and soon you'll see how fun meditation and breath work can be.

Take a monster breath like Mantra.

Breathe through your nose and hold your breath for

1 2 3 4.

Then let it out with a monster roar for

8 7 6 5 4 3 2 1.

ROOOOAAAR!

Breathe in one way and out the next, now you're taking a monster breath.

Are you having a stormy day?
Mantra says blow it away.

Take a big breath in

.... and **BLOW** the cloud away.

Repeat until your storm cloud has gone away.

Grab your breathing buddy and set him on your stomach.
Watch him rise as you fill your belly up with air
1 2 3 4 5 6

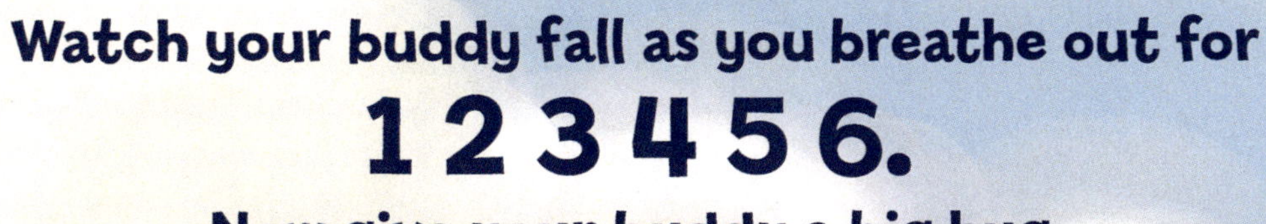

Watch your buddy fall as you breathe out for
1 2 3 4 5 6.
Now give your buddy a big hug.

Breath
Breathe

Place your finger on Mantra's friends.
Breathe in through your nose until you reach Mantra.
Then breathe out as you reach Mantra's friends.
Repeat until you feel calm and happy.

10
Mantra says close your eyes.
Mantra says dream of skies.
Mantra says rest your head.
Mantra says count to ten.
Now it's time to go to bed.

A Parents Guide to Meditation

Meditation: Is a practice where an individual uses a technique - such as mindfulness, or focusing the mind on a particular object, thought, or activity - to train attention and awareness, and achieve a mentally clear and emotionally calm and stable state.

Mindfulness: A mental state achieved by focusing one's awareness on the present moment, while calmly acknowledging and accepting one's feelings, thoughts, and bodily sensations, used as a therapeutic technique.

Breath work: A New Age term for various breathing practices in which the conscious control of breathing is said to influence a person's mental, emotional or physical state, with a claimed therapeutic effect.

Mantra: A mantra or mantram is a sacred utterance, a numinous sound, a syllable, word or phonemes, or group of words in Sanskrit, Pali and other languages believed by practitioners to have religious, magical or spiritual powers. Some mantras have a syntactic structure and literal meaning, while others do not.

Inner peace: Is defined as the state of physical and spiritual calm despite many stressors. To find your peace of mind means finding happiness, contentment, and bliss no matter how hard you go through in life.

About the Author

Taylor grew up in Chicago where her enthusiasm for mental health and overall wellness flourished. Taylor is a psychologist with a love for inspiring the next generation of readers. She lives in southern California with her husband, son and two fur babies.

Made in the USA
Las Vegas, NV
01 December 2021